The Dedalus Press

__Making Space__

Francis Harvey

Collections of poetry by Francis Harvey:

"In the Light on the Stones", Gallery Press 1978
"The Rainmakers", Gallery Press 1988
"The Boa Island Janus", Dedalus Press 1996

MAKING SPACE

NEW & SELECTED POEMS

FRANCIS HARVEY

Dublin 2001

The Dedalus Press, 24 The Heath, Cypress Downs, Dublin 6W. Ireland

visit www.dedaluspoetry.com

ISBN 1 901233 74 X (paper)
ISBN 1 901233 75 8 (bound)

Cover Painting by Lawson Burch

Acknowledgements:
to the Gallery Press for permission to reprint poems originally pu b-
lished in "In the Light on the Stones" and "The Rainmakers". Some
of the poems, or versions of them, in the last section, first appeared
in: *Poetry Ireland Review, Metre, Céide, Force 10, Honest Ulsterman, Or
Volge L'Anno/At the Year's Turning* (Dedalus)

Dedalus Press books are represented and distributed in the
U.S.A. and Canada by Dufour Editions Ltd., P.O. Box 7,
Chester Springs, Pennsylvania 19425
and in the UK by Central Books, 99 Wallis Road, London E9
5LN

The Dedalus Press receives financ ial assistance from
An Chomhairle Ealaíon, The Arts Council, Ireland.

Contents:

:

from *The Boa Island Janus*

New Poems

FROM *IN THE LIGHT ON THE STONES*

DEATH OF THADY

He could not tell you why
he loves the place so much — and
love's a word that he would never use.

He could not tell you why
there is no other place where
he walks taller than Errigal
and plants his feet like dolmens
in a wind-scoured land of scant grass and scanter sky.

He could not tell you why,
when he lay ailing in the warm bright ward,
the dark glens and the lonely
lakes in the sky and the flagged
cabin cold and bare as a prison-cell,
were heaven to him as sure as this was hell.

He could not tell you why,
after the priest had gone
and the nurse indifferently watched him die,
he suddenly saw the hill-wind swirling
the turf-mould on the ward-room floor
and counted the last of his sheep filing
like mourners through the gap of the door.

AN EARLY SPACEMAN

They make a space for him who inhabits space
as a star inhabits the loneliness of it.
He stands on his own at the back of the thronged hall,
a long great-coat corded round the cairn of his body.
He steams in the heat and a pool of dampness gathers
about him and the sheepdog lying at his feet.
The peaked cap's a fungus growing out of his head,
the black rubber boots are bollards of eroded peat.
He lights up with hunched shoulders, huge hands cupped
round the bowl of the pipe, the sound of the wind that matts
wisps of the Grey Mare's Tail on the haunches of Suhill
whorled in his ears for ever like the sea in a shell.
Smoke clouds the weathered granite of his face.
Suddenly the dog pricks up its ears, watching
his lips, waiting for a signal from him
to rout this pen of bleating sheep good
for neither dipping nor shearing.
But its master dreams, has a rapt faraway
look in his eyes as if already nostalgic for
the vast acreage of sky outside. He's calculating
the price he should get for his ewes at Brockagh Fair.

ELEGY FOR THE ISLANDERS

They died elsewhere but their graves are here
and these bare gables are their head-stones.

Their strong hearts faltered long before their
roof-beams fell and their hearth-stones, cold

as their bones in an alien earth, mourn the memory
of their fires in diamonds of black.

I walk on the lichened stones of their graves
and a split flag cracks as their hearts cracked

once. I hear their death-rattles deep down
in the gullet of the sound and taste the salt

of their tears on the wind. Tears will wear out
a stone but what will a heart wear out but itself?

They wore out their hearts and left nothing here
but stones washed by the tides of their tears.

MANUS

Was it for this
he enriched her body with a spendthrift
abandon his lean acres craved in lime
yet broke her on a standing stone
as hard and inexorable as Time?

Was it for this
he took crop his loins had sown
on flesh and bone and shipped it overseas
like bags of Banner seed, then limed the land
too late for beasts no son of his would need?

Was it for this
he cast her, spent as a kelt, alongside
the corpse of her stillborn tenth child
and hardened his heart against the knife of a wind
sharper than March hones on the hills of Disert?

Was it for this
he tholed the gnawing teeth of the seasons
that stripped his spirit to the bone until
it was as cold as a granite boulder
the glacier once scoured out of Gaguin?

To stand alone
in his doorway at nightfall and watch, high above
dewfall and hawkfall, the sky seeded with stars
as barren as he wished in Christ's name his own
seed had been all the times he'd opened her for another lost crop.

AN OAK IN THE GLEN

He is ploughing
the lea field
with the brown mare
the way
his father and
his father's father
ploughed it;

he is taking
the burn hill
under a streamer of gulls
the way
his father and
his father's father
took it;

he is stooping
under a yoke
heavier than his mare's
the way
that stunted oak
stoops in the wind
from the sea;

the way
it was stooped
in the wind
from the sea
when his father
and his father's father
ploughed this lea;

the way
it will still be stooped
in the wind
from the sea
when his children and
his children's children
plough this lea.

IN MEMORY OF PATRICK MACGILL 1890-1963

Childhood was the rainbow you knew would end
for good at the foot of the glen. Over-
night Strabane made a man of you the hard
way; no more crocks of gold then. You'd sold your
body to the highest bidder but your spirit
would always be inviolate to grosser men;
the best thing you could do now was
to put it all down in words: glensmen
cast like seed on the four winds;
the magic in the light at certain times
of day; those hills full of lakes, sheep, silence;
the rushy holms stippled with sunlight and flowers;
Christ on your lips at Mass; the chrism
of wonder transfiguring every stone and
blade of grass until they became a part
of you ever after in Glasgow, London,
the trenches, New York.

When you died in exile years later were
the fibres and splinters still festering in your heart?

17

BRENDAN IN DONEGAL

He could forget the malice of cities:
Whispered knives in his back on every street:
London, Paris, New York, Dublin: pities
And glories still triggering heart and feet.

For him, each evening, rainbows arched our skies,
The glens were blue-belled, magpies flew in pairs;
Tinkers and sheepmen eyed him with surprise:
A ribald cherub sampling country airs.

He came on tidal waves of talk; the moor,
Island, quay, and pub, our native sounds, were drowned
In saltier seas; and when he left we found

The certain marks of a leviathan.
But the first trippers, stumbling on the spoor
Of genius, showed us the footprints of a man.

IN THE LIGHT ON THE STONES IN THE RAIN

Mostly, in West Donegal,
it is rock and light, and water, but rock above all,
and rain, to-day it is rain, rain falling softly in veils
on foxglove and fuchsia and furze;
and, plaintively calling all day by the sea,
in the mist and the spray,
back and forth in the rain wheel the birds,
plover and curlew and teal.
And then there are men,
in the light on the stones in the rain,
sometimes men, but not often,
for mostly in West Donegal
it is rock and light, and water, not men,
and to-day, to-day it is rain, rain falling softly in veils
on foxglove and fuchsia and furze,
and on birds.

GATES

We're a people who do not love gates, we
are lovers of gaps,
all sorts of oddly-shaped gaps,
gaps in the crochet of lime-stone walls,
gaps in the clouds and the hills,
we are lovers of space,
and our only concession to gates is
a bush or a broken old bed
that creaks in the wind from the Croaghs.
And that's as it should be —-
except for the fact that, me,
at times I get tired and I like what I see
so much — a gap with a twenty-mile view to the sea —
I feel I could do with a rest for a while,
just something to lean on and stare —
and a gate, for example, would do.
That's all we think they are good for.

MAP LICHEN ON SLIEVETOOEY

Up on this bare summit
where fierce weathers pare
heather and peat down
to its skeletal bone
until the cairns groan
like gods in labour
I check my route and
watch a hare white
in its winter coat sit
back in a gap of light
scaning a stone whose
lichen maps
worlds
unknown to me and
cartography.

Snow

We woke this winter's day to snow
brimming the room with light
and silence and rose to a world
of white perfection: a tree furred with
ermine, a row of icicles barbing the eave-run
of the barn, the sun on a fleece of immaculate
lawn tracked with a bird's italics.

INFORMATION FOR TOURISTS

Pull up your car for a moment, stranger,
look hard at that broken discarded man
who totters on sticks between the mountain
and the sea. Once he was strong and upright
as you or me till, scraping in the scraw
of his few acres here at home or tatie-
hoking in an icy Scottish mist
from dawn to dusk took all the sweetness
out of him and left this husk. He shares his crust
with no one now, his wife a rickle of misshapen
bones under thin salt clay and stone, his seed,
seed of his loins that didn't fall on barren
Rosses rock and soil, long borne on bitter tides
of grief into the ghettos of half-a-dozen
capital cities and never his own.
Remember Thady when your camera whirrs
on seascape and empty glen, for he too played some part,
who let them make this place a playground for you
out of his desolation of heart.

23

DALLAS: THE NIGHTMARE FRONTIER

He rode into the scrublands of that last
Frontier unarmed against such lawless law.
On every trail unsaddled stallions passed
Him, wild-eyed, screaming; at noon he saw

The lynched sheriff's enormous shadow swing
Across the sun; wagons of liquor, guns,
Inflamed the tribes, while the last posse hung
Back and watched the ritual slaughter of its sons.

Brazen on every street the killers stood
Jingling their spurs like bangled whores; the court-
House blazed, the judge was shot, and one report

Spoke of another scalping in the South —
Until a new assassin mapped in blood
Darker frontiers where Babel shuts Truth's mouth.

SWIFT

Was it that *education of a dog*
Unfitted him to ape those suaver wits
Settling for slippered sex and gout? Some rich bog-
Trotting bishop's only child prone to fits

Of gloom? Formalities of love and hate
He mocked passionately, fearing passion's
Incandescence in the child-menaced state
Of marriage, haunted by dark compassions.

A greater master ruled whose irony
Was final: Time's sane children spoke, acclaimed
The claw-marked prose as magical, then tamed,

Embraced this tiger like a nursery toy,
And when it snarled some raw obscenity
Appalled their parents with their shrieks of joy.

PATRICK KAVANAGH

Steam from the Mucker dung-heap mists his mind
In Baggot street, condensing into dreams
Of innocence in haunted fields. The wind
That shakes the bed-head in the gap streams

From the stars and God will seed the spirit
With it yet. The pits in winter rise like mounds
To buried kings; the mire and clobber set
Hard with frost; and over the hill the sound

Of Markey's cart jolting in frozen ruts pulls
At the heart. And girls are roses in the light
Of lime-washed walls and still the fiend each night

Breaks loose into the crotch of death and drools till day
Re-yokes the ploughman to the broken earth and gulls,
Like angels round his head, acclaim the clay.

A Picked Bone

The wet limestone
pitted
by sea and rain
and the tears of exiles
glitters
like broken glass in a sudden
avalanche of light that melts
the mist from the glistening
crevice-flowers and strips
the great-breasted
hills up to the very tips
of their nipples where
the hawk has it all
to himself now as he sits
on the wind and broods
on his shadow and
the mouse he will shortly
kill as it waits by the weed-
choked hearth of the roofless
house for the crumbs that will
never come;
the hawk has it all
to himself now as craw-full
at dusk he drifts down-wind
over an island plucked
clean of people
as a stone or
a picked bone.

THE CAUL
for Pauline

You came up in the doctor's trawl that day:
you and your twin sister in the same net:
fish out of water, drowning in air, two
spring-run six-pound salmon, slippery, wet.

But *you* were born with a caul on your head,
a lucky charm against drowning at sea.
Before you touched the deck the doctor had
your birth-cap promised to Nahor the Quay.

Sometimes when we're sailing to the islands
and the half-decker lurches in a squall
I look at you and wish we'd kept that cap:
once is enough to come up in a trawl.

AT ARDS

All day the pheasants were honking
like vintage cars and
the cows cropped
young grass with a sound
of rending cloth. The ferns
were uncurling their croziers under
the candelabra of the chestnuts and
the hills were blue, blue
as the pools of bluebells in the grass. There was
a smell of crushed
almonds in the airs eddying
from the whins
and you were there
with a flower in your hand and I
was with you and I wanted
to take your other hand but
the children were there
as well and the cows.
I knew they would stare.

AT ARDS AGAIN
for Joan

Walking all day in the woods with you,
mile after mile with nothing to say,
except to show you the April beeches

budded with talons like birds of prey;
walking all day through the pines and birches,
mile after mile in the sun and the rain,

what can I say at the end of the journey
but when will we walk in the woods again,
mile after mile with nothing to say?

A SAPLING BIRCH

You have grown out of our reach:
a seed sown long ago now
tall as this sapling birch. I
measure the infinite distance:
fingers of wind in the leaves like
my hands in your hair; a misty
April dawn resonant with bird-
song; our bedroom and the stranger
we welcomed there. So much you
owe to love's climate of kiss
and touch, the soil that nourished you,
the embracing light: remember this.
I hand you over to your lover now
to grow a seedling out of that good earth.
Grow it, grow it and let us rejoice
that you have grown out of our reach.
Out of the good earth grow a sapling birch.

ELEGY FOR A ROBIN

Something that doesn't belong up here any
more lies on its back in the grass down there.
This tiny foreign body is clogging
the bitter currents of boisterous winter air.

A berry of blood has congealed on its beak
like a haw on this hedge now out of its reach
and I think of all those birds long dead whose songs
sweetened my songs before I soured into speech.

O cold this breeze that plumped its feathers once
and now stirs a claw thin as a filament.
I shiver but *live* in these alien fields.
Only the dead are out of their element.

THE LAST DROVER

For fifty years he travelled light into
every kind of darkness and saw more
winter dawns than was good for man or beast.

He wore the same serge suit summer
and winter indifferent as a whin bush
to the wind and rain that bent him in the end.

He slept on his feet like them listening
for the silences that woke him when
they softened through a gap or

bunched in sudden terror of a shadow.
He knew the stones of his roads better
than the corns on his feet.

Their heat warmed him on bitter nights.
They lowed to their own kind across stone walls and ditches.
He talked out loud to himself in the dark.

I mourn him now who left no deeds or songs
to set against the curlew's desolating cry at dawn,
who left no deeds or songs at all.

FROM *THE RAINMAKERS*

THE RAINMAKERS
for Esther

We shake the young birches
hung with fat raindrops:
local showers that drench
only you and me; witch
doctors, I know, do it
better but this is
personal rainmaking,
private weather. Listen
to the laughter of myself
and my daughter under
the dripping birches.

LOUGH ESKE WOOD : THE BLUE MIST

Nothing much ever happens up here
in the stones and grass: a nondescript brambly
place full of saplings of hazel and ash,
you could pass it for most of the year with
barely a glance. Of course, if you really
fancied the place enough, you could sit there all day
in the sun and the rain and a ram-lamb
or ewe-lamb might dance you a jig
on the grass to the tune of a bird, or
a pheasant might crow, or the wind from the sea grow
lonely listening to the sound of its own
lonely voice. Nothing much ever happens
up here, as I say, until one day
of sun and shadows maybe, looking up through the trees,
you stand transfixed to see in the distance
a blue mist shimmering and floating in the breeze
as veil after veil of bluebells tremulously dare
to match the new shade of Spring a shower's
just washed into the May skies.

THE DEAF WOMAN IN THE GLEN

for Robert Bernen

In her own silence
in the silence
of the glen she is

a stone accepting
rain, a thorn bent
under the weight

of the wind, a heap
of bleached bones
in the gullet

of a dry burn. She has
hair whiter than
Scardan has in

winter; feldspar is
the pink grained
in the granite

of her cheeks; clouds
shadow the unplumbed
peat-brown

of her eyes and, perched
on this outcrop
of rock outside her

door and native
to her station as
the raven to its

crag, she is
locked in this
landscape's fierce

embrace as
the badger is whose
unappeasable jaws only

death unlocks from
the throat of rabbit
or rat and

moves, free yet
tethered, through
Time's inexorable weathers

in her solitary orbit
of the silent spaces
under the haunches

of her mountains and
the grey distended
udder of the sky.

A SNOWY GOOD FRIDAY

I take the snowy lakeside road today
past ice-frilled reeds that rustle in the sun
like cellophane; two stiff-necked whoopers eye
me from afar; the cold inflates a robin
on a white-capped stone and everywhere
the snow reveals the secret lives of men
and beasts: who would have thought, for instance, that
both fox and hare so much frequented this
bare place among the whins and rocks; that John
has twice already crossed this field today
with fodder from that haystack on his back
and stood, like me, under this overhang
to watch his steaming Friesians eat their fill
of hay that once was grass and flowers rooted
in the earth beneath their feet; who would have thought
that I was not the first to bowl pine cones
across the frozen shallows of the lake
and pit the drum-tight ice with fusillades
of stones like any vandal tempted by
a pane of glass?
                              The boles of trees and poles
and fencing posts are piped with ermine down
one side and sheep I thought last week were white
stand dazed and lost in dazzling drifts of light
as if bewildered by a landscape that
they thought they knew until it changed itself
into something as utterly strange and
new as that commonplace threadbare scrap
of daylight moon up there does night after night.
A wisp of wild geese in the distance fades
like wind-blown smoke; the woods are full of small
mysterious sounds as snow that fell
as silently as light now melts in tears
it sheds for Him whose death it mourned in white.

41

BLESSINGS

Yesterday, for some reason I couldn't
understand, I suddenly felt starved
of trees and had to make tracks towards
the beeches of Lough Eske to set my heart
at ease and stand there slowly adjusting
myself to the overwhelming presence of all
those trees. It was like coming back among
people again after living for ages
alone and as I reached out and laid my
right hand in blessing on the trunk
of a beech that had the solidity but not
the coldness of stone I knew it for
the living thing it was under the palm
of my hand as surely as I know the living
sensuousness of flesh and bone and my
blessing was returned a hundredfold
before it was time for me to go home.

THE SINNER AND THE SNOW IN THE GLEN

The first crocuses are
candle flames among
the starched altar-cloths
of late snow; the gate pier's

surpliced; under
a crucifix of weeping ice
nunneries of snow-
drops bow their heads,

pendulous and heavy
as thuribles; blood-red,
huge, the sanctuary
lamp hangs over Carn

on a faint chain of stars;
white inviolate aisles
creak under my feet
and the weight of my sins.

ON LEAHAN

Another year has gone bv since we heard the voices.
Innocence grows harder and harder to find
and death has taken its customary toll.
You have acquired your first grey hair.
Today as I climb the mountain in drifts of rain
the sea sends up its smoke-signals among the rocks,
the season for orchids has long since passed
and the ferns in the scree have begun to turn
into traceries of rusted wrought-iron filigree.
Points of mercurial light dance on the horizon.
I remember how on the summit that day
we heard the voices of playing children calling
out to one another in a language neither of us
had ever heard before and may never hear again.
We searched and searched but found no one:
not even the print of minuscule feet
in the soft black rain-pitted peat. Then the voices
faded away.

I have come here alone today to listen
once more but I have heard nothing except
the song of the wind in the rib-cage of a dead sheep,
the crying of curlews in the rain,
and now in the pub hours afterwards a man
tells me of someone who claims to have heard
the same voices we heard that day.
He speaks in a serious matter-of-fact way
like someone discussing the price of houses or cars.
I know I'll come back. Again and again. I might even
try to pick up some of the language.

UNDINE AND THE SEAL

for Anthony Glavin

He treads water to get
a better view of you:
the bald wet

dogshead gleams like
sunlit wrack: the eyes
are soulful

as my bitch's but
I know it is a bull —
the thick fat

neck of him; the bulge
of that brutal profile — rising
up to watch the wind

lick your body into shape:
cleft of bivalve, soft-
shelled limpets

of your breasts, the caves
Love will as surely fathom
as this seal

fathoms the cavernous
mysteries of the sea
again and again.

A LITTLE THING

She married late: an islandman who reeked
of fish and turfsmoke; the sea was on his
lips and in his kisses. She liked that
and in bed at night she liked listening to the way
the Gaelic suddenly came spurting
out of him the same time as his seed. A little
thing she missed: the trees of home, evenings
of splintered light, a net of shadows tangling
and untangling on the grass. He said
that she was mad, that others had tried and failed,
but she went on and now she has this stump
of hawthorn and a stunted sycamore
too low to ever tangle with the light.
Nothing will coax an inch more out of them.
She hates their sickly look. He laughs.
I told you so. A tree will never grow out here.
And kisses her to sweeten what he says.
She tastes the bitterness of salt.

IN MEMORY OF PATRICK BOYLE 1905-1982

It was snowing in Glenveagh the day you
died, Moylenanav was white, and the red
deer watched us through fluted curtains of flowered
light; the torrents were writhing like serpents
in the heather and the waterfalls hung
out of the sky like the entrails of clouds;
the wind was skinning the boles of birches
and peeling the scabs of lichen
from the scalps of the stones and we were cold
that day as we ate our brown bread and cheese
under a dripping rhododendron
but not as cold as you were, Patrick Boyle, had
we known it then, laid out on your bed
on the far side of Ireland.
                          The deer turned their
beautiful buff-coloured rumps
into the wind and one stag with antlers twisting
out of its head like a thornbush
out of a split crag paused for a moment to stare
at us out of eyes as impenetrable
and mysterious as the wilderness
in which it was bred.
                         I remembered those
eyes when they told me, Patrick Boyle, that you
were dead and how you looked at me that last
time I saw you alive with the eyes
of a stag being hunted towards the ultimate
wilderness for which we are all bred.

WITTGENSTEIN

For years, deciding that he knew it all,
he switched to simpler, less demanding arts
until, discovering that he might be wrong,
he found that language determines how things are,
an element, not a precision tool,
something mind inhabits, a bird in air,
the fish of logic in a verbal pool,
and, boring some student from his wooden chair,
did he make him wonder if, alone in rooms
or silent for hours with Russell thinking
of sin and logic, there might not be *someone* who,
like Carmen or Betty, transcending
the limits of logic, reason, art,
could teach him the private language of the heart?

THE YOUNG CURATE

He lived alone till she arrived and she
is one of them: a sheepman's widow
without child, soft and shapeless as a ewe
at shearing, her tongue barbed as one
of their fences. In the flagged kitchen at night
he hears their sing-song voices — English
uneasily riding the Gaelic undertow —
often the low growl of a dog.
He sees them sometimes silently filing
along the gravelled path towards
the kitchen door like sheep along
a mountain track. She feeds him well but leaves
him to himself: this is a world of men,
dogs and women come when summoned.
A sick call and she's up and out before
him to the hall and gossiping with
someone — as if death too could wait like
this man standing, cap in hand, inside
the door. In time he will grow used
to almost everything — the solitude,
the sparsity of trees, the reek of turfsmoke
from his clothes — everything except the way,
perfumed and fur-coated for the weekly
shopping trip to town, she settles
herself into the front seat of his car
like a clocking hen on a clutch of eggs.

CONDY AT EIGHTY

Going to sleep at night sometimes he
imagines he hears the cries
of young girls but wakes at dawn

to the bleating of sheep in the rain.
The wind has spared one sycamore but
each year sap still rises in it;

in summer it holds out the palms
of its hands to a miserly sun.
When he prays or swears the words

come in Irish: roots are the last
to die. If he had ever made love
the words would have come that way

too. The silence of the glen is
the silence at the bottom
of the sea; he has been drowning in it

for as long as he can remember:
a slow death. No one
understands his cries for help: it

is a private language he shares
with God and his dogs. The beds
of the torrents are paved with broken

stones from the heart of the mountain
and the light breaks loose from the clouds
like a wild thing; soon it is trapped

in shadows. In eight years these
granite hills can break a working
dog. It took longer to break him.

THE WRITING ROOM

So much of his life was spent in this room
full of books, this mortuary for a heart
and mind embalmed, this sparsely-furnished tomb,
where, sounding the shallows and the depths, he charts

the wrecks of love silted up in marriage.
Nothing ever *happened* in this room.
What happened happened elsewhere in a rage
of love and hate: in the tiled kitchen's gloom

where the cat curled up at the fire or a bee
trapped in a web indifferently eyed
another fire blaze as she and he
watched on TV how love was born and died.

Or in that red-carpeted upstairs room
where no one saw them shaping up to doom.

LETTING GO
for Gerard Moriarty

He came today to take away her things
(I'm glad I wasn't there to see them go):
blouses and dresses, lingerie and rings,
even that tattered doll minus its toe.

I know we have to let them live their lives.
Not even love can change a thing like that.
Live and let live it was and it survived
the dramas of her love life and her hats.

But something deeper warns us to let go,
one of those things we never put in words.
Out of the darkness sunlit flowers grow,
under the silken cloak scabbards and swords.

Lives are for living: she must live her own.
The mystery of love is flesh and bone.

BLUE

There's someone burning scrub down by the lake.
We smell the tang of it among the trees
and hear the crackle and the spit before
we glimpse blue smoke thinning in the breeze.

I wish I knew why things like woodsmoke
stir you so; I wish I knew the reason why
I am always losing you, as I lose
you suddenly now, to the blue of the sky

and the blue Bord Fáilte mountain in the lake
and all the blue translucencies of smoke
that dream such dreams of blueness in your eyes
you would not waken even if I spoke.

DEATH

We climbed all day through inundations
and inundations of light
until the islands shrank

in size to stepping stones across a burn.
Cloud shadows broke wild as March hares
over the screes; thick wet

lips of peat bared the stones of their teeth
at us; the wind combed partings white as bone
in your hair.

And then I saw the falcon fall from the sky:
arc after dark arc slicing the incandescent light;
I held my breath.

He nearly took you once: your grazed face
white as a tooth or a bone
under that fierce stoop.

THE HAIRS OF HER HEAD
for my brother, Michael

The nuns had cut her hair the day before
and now these outraged eyes in a white cropped
felon's head that scarcely dents the pillow bored
like gimlets into mine. *You* should have stopped

them doing this to me is what they said,
and said until she died — as if aware,
like Samson, of all the strength that
lay in the glory of her much-cherished hair

that was waist-long that childhood day she was
drowning in the Erne and black as her boots
as her sister grabbed and held on though she could see
strands of it snapping close to the roots.

All that's left of it now is upstairs, locked,
with her trinkets and things, in a box.

THE ASHPLANT

For ages, buried in dusty bric-à-brac
and toys, it lay unnoticed in the lumber-
room until one night his tarmacadam
driveway rang with the thud of hooves and
heavy breathing sounds he hadn't heard
for thirty years. He ran outside and found this
bullock shying at its shadow on a wall
and four more lipping tulips on the lawn;
one roared and tossed its head in panic, sand-
wiched between the Escort and the Merc. He shooed
and semaphored, shouted and shook his pipe
at them, but they ignored this dervish
in his pin-stripe suit until suddenly he
thought of it and rushed inside and dug
it from its grave and, facing them across
a bed of trampled flowers and waving it,
he felt the magic come and watched them melt
back into the darkness where a barefoot boy
is standing near a wizened little man
in torn serge trousers and a knitted cap,
an ashplant like a sceptre in his hand
and at his back the kingdom of bog and rock
his son had flogged to German millionaires
before he was cold in Malin sand and stone.

WEATHERS

Slieve League's marbled with February snow
but larks are warming up here at its base.
Waves of unreal light break over sheep and cows.
The sea's white with acres of billowing lace.

The mountain inverts itself in the sky
in the lake, two different shades of blue.
A sea mist wears itself threadbare on stone.
Its lining of sky begins to show through,

you stride ahead into a cloud's shadow.
The dog's sniffing at some bones and feathers.
I follow. The way I have followed you
now for thirty years in all weathers.

JOHN CLARE
for Madge Herron

I am eye-level with harebells
and bees on a swelling curve
of the earth. The wind breathes
on the nape of my neck. I exchange
the integument of my body
for the pelt of the grass; beetles
and ladybirds inhabit the interstices
of my bones, explore the valves
of my heart. I insert my fingers
into the moist orifices of earth,
bruise my lips on clay and stones.
The swish of birds' wings brushes
against my ears like the silken
passage of girls in long dresses.
I enter the secret places
where worms turn the world
on their shoulders and pass the earth
through the alembic of their guts.
In the labyrinth of the green
forest I find them: a hare's foot,
horseshoes, a rainbow of lichen.
Someone calls me. The keeper comes,
trampling the light underfoot,
speaking a familiar language
I am trying to unlearn.
His words clash with the pealing
of birds, the tongued bells of flowers.

FROM *THE BOA ISLAND JANUS*

IDENTITIES

Fermanagh: half in and half out
of whatever its element is,
never quite sure at any time

whether it's one thing or the other,
land in water or water in land,
but amphibious like me amid

the fluencies and insularities that
lie even deeper than land or water and
host here in this graveyard by the lake

among the tussocked and hummocked graves
of Boa Island's Christian dead
to a squat twin-headed stone idol

that was looking two ways long before
I knew there were two ways of looking
upstream to a source and downstream to the sea.

LOVE LETTERS

H.M.H. The mustered consonants stand
to attention like soldiers on the page:
no surrender to the insidious
mellifluous importunities
of the songs the siren orchestrates
out of a, e, i, o, u. From the seduction
of vowels, Lord, deliver your consonants
and know your own by the sound of their names.

O'Shea, O'Flaherty, McHugh and McCool:
names that could hardly have been more than names
to him — not people they'd ever invite
to afternoon tea — until she came
vowelling like a swallow from the South
and melted every consonant in his mouth.

ICONS

He used to lift me high above his head
like a football trophy until I was
eye-level with the cardboard print she'd nailed
above the fanlight in the hall. And when
I'd fall back into his arms, helpless with laughter,
and feel the sandpaper of his beard
against my cheek I'd suddenly smell
him and draw him deep down into my lungs

until I was drugged with love for him and
for the cobwebbed Christ I was too young to
understand my father must have thought such
a strange thing there. As strange as those pictures
of the King and Queen I used to see
in the houses of his people were to me.

CANCER

It was what I expected it would be
but for the smells: their rankness took my breath
away. They led me by the hand from cage
to cage. A monkey yawned and ate its fleas,
the reptiles slept, dreaming of sin and death,
a baby cried. I saw the lions and
the elephant and heard the parrots rage
all through that afternoon and felt a vague

mysterious sense of something going on
beyond what was going on here: a world I'd
sometimes glimpsed when for no reason at all
grown-ups would suddenly burst into tears
or kiss or, like my parents now, constantly
reach out to touch each other and touch me.

THE SPACE BETWEEN

I used to help her make her bed that time.
I'd plump and pummel the bolster and pillows
back into shape again and smooth the rucks
and creases out of blankets and sheets
with the palms of my hands. I'd face her
with nothing between us but the ease of our
silence and the white lonely reaches she'd
now been abandoned to dream in alone

and I'd snap and billow the sheets until
I could feel the pulse and pull of her coming
through to me from the other end like love
trying to keep in touch when the lines
were still open and the space between us
no more than the width of a double bed.

67

THE LANGUAGE BOG

You learned to pick your steps from stone to stone:
one false move and you could get bogged down
in what for you was treacherous ground you were
only beginning to find your way through
by circuitous routes and in disguise.
You were barefooted and unsure but they
knew exactly where they were going and,
dryshod, kept passing you out on the way.

We kept them to ourselves: contraband
it could be dangerous to declare: those words
we took out like love letters or keepsakes
when we were alone or with our kin,
confession, benediction, chapel, nun,
sure-footed now as sheep on their own ground.

THE WHEELWRIGHT AND THE BOY

In memory of James Orr

Even then I thought of him as Joseph
the Worker ankle-deep in shavings
of oak and ash — as though he'd been snipping
curls from blond heads of crepitant hair all
day long and this was a barber's shop.
I saw the shape of the felloes in his stoop
at the bench, knots in the wood when effort
made the veins in his hands bunch and stand out.

I was a cross he had to bear: always
touching things and asking questions about
the icons of the maker: spokeshaves, awls,
planes, gouges, chisels, saws, all those names for
the mystery of love and how it works
even when it's working against the grain.

VOYAGERS

Summers we went west to Donegal and
wonders: a farm between two waterfalls
in sight of mountains and the sea, the all-
night-long cacophony of corncrakes in
the meadow that was his pride and joy as
I'd set course for sleep by the open window.
The curtains would fill with wind like sails and
swish and billow until I'd feel I was

under way like a ship, and I was too,
I suppose, not like him lying next door
whose long voyage was drawing to a close
now and whose muffled laments would sometimes
reach me like a fogbound coaster calling
for a pilot at the mouth of the lough.

NEWS OF THE WORLD

Time had beached him like a stranded whale
on the bleak shores of a big brass bed. The past
sang to him: the sea in a shell. I
was his lookout at the window of the upstairs
room. He'd cup his hand round his ear
when I'd call out to him how many cows
Stinson was grazing on the long acre now.
I'd listen to news of a world he knew
long before I knew there was a world to know.

And so it would go on, with him left
high and dry and out of his element by the tide
and me all eyes for the eyes that always
seemed to be looking beyond me
at things I'd never be able to see.

THE MYTH MAKER

The days of cattle-raiding dawn campaigns
to Connaught fairs were epics of the past;
he'd fallen amongst women now, and when
they'd leave me looking after him, and he'd
no more to say, we'd listen to the river
finding its voice down at the Falls. I liked
that and I liked the sense of being at ease

with someone who, resting at last from deeds,
disarmed, in bed, was equally at ease
with me as I shaped him into someone
as heroic and legendary as
Cathleen or Red Hugh who gave their names to
waterfalls they'd all be astonished now
to find no longer there to listen to.

THE SEEDBED

In memory of William Allingham

Even though it lay fallow for years now,
the big bed he found himself floundering through
these days knew all there was to know
about sowing seed. But she was years dead
and he, with the crop he'd once raised raising
crops of their own now, was well past planting
anything more than a word in your ear.
The right word at the right time it turned out

as seed he never even knew he'd sown,
or had it in him to sow, took root and
grew when he was long gone. I'm still
taking crop from the field. The one he tilled
for that townsman of his whose poetry   ·
he used broadcast across the bed to me.

IN THE MEADOW

We were standing a good bit apart
on the grass at the end of another day of

perfect weather. You were dressed for indoors
as you usually were and not for outside

and you looked a bit out-of-place and lost
as you always did in an open space —

even here in one of your father's fields.
We were watching them winching the last

of the trampcocks up the tilted deck of
the shifter but what we were really watching

was watching nothing at all. The cloud
shadows took ages to pass that day and

the tracks of the horse-drawn shifter shone like
ribbons of tinfoil in the crushed green plush

of the aftergrass and I don't have to tell
you what we were saying or what passed between us

because we said nothing and nothing at all
passed between us as we stood there a good bit

apart in a dream on the grass at the end
of another day of perfect weather

drawing closer and closer together.

HERON

In memory of Beatrice Behan

was assembled out of bits and scraps, not made.
Like one of those early flying machines held together
       with glue and twine.
His undercarriage is an afterthought sticking out behind.
He is all wings and no fuselage and probably hollow inside.
Finn could have blown him off the palm of his hand.

He creaks into flight. The wind buffets him, gives him
a bumpy ride: it seems he must somehow end up
in a twisted heap of canvas and struts on the mountainside.
But no: he tacks into weathers with a prow that rises
       and falls in the swell.
The ghost of the pterodactyl haunts him in every cell.

He alights: furls his wings like a wet umbrella, settles,
       rapt and murderous,
drying out in the wind and sun on the edge of a tarn
or hunched over a pool in the burn pretending he's
a blind one-legged beggarman or a mystic
       communing with God.
Too late, too late for the fish or frog when it realises
       he's not an old cod.

Heron invented slow motion long before the movies came but
allows himself the lightning of his pickaxe
       for the killing game.
Heron's the icon of the silences beyond the last tongues
of land where the islands float and quiver like mirages
       in the light,
he's the hermit who daily petrifies himself in the reeds
       of the penitential lake,

the logo of the lonely places past the last sheep and
        the last house,
the El Greco or Modigliani doodle in a remote corner
        of the evening sky where
the newsprint of distant waders swims before the eye,
heron's that sudden outlandish screech you hear at midnight
in the water meadows as he changes into the wrong gear.

BRIAN'S HOUSE

The glen was full of barking dogs but you
kept none: you'd sold out to the forestry
years ago and had no need of one, and so
in time the hill behind your house has
darkened with trees and the shadows of trees
and your old stamping ground, where you ran
a few score of black-face ewes until
arthritis tethered you to the half-circle
round your front door, now nourishes nothing
but the roots of conifers. Last week
on a day as warm as that summer's day
the two of us sat on the drystone wall
outside your door chatting for ages about
how some things in life go right, some wrong,
and how so much that was good has now gone,
last week I came that way again past
the barking dogs and the wind-scoured farms
of the people of the glen and past the house
that once had no dog and now has no man.

SHEEPMEN

The dog noses a steaming bag lumped
like an afterbirth at the open door.
Two kittens eye the *danse macabre*
of a leaf impaled on a thorn and the sky
is wet whitewash. God knows when it will dry.
What scarecrow's that an insidious wind
has stretched out on the broad of its back
in the furrowed reaches of the big brass bed?
Whose claws are those endlessly fondling
the folds of the bedclothes with a passion
never lavished on human flesh and bone?
Whose eyes are those that keep turning away from
the sparse light outside to the sparser light within?
Owen McSharry of Crieve is on his rack.
Today he waits for the priest to come creaking
up the narrow stairs past the hired woman
and the Sacred Heart picture on the wall
with the body of Christ in a box.
A sheepman like himself and the only one
he'd trust to rid him of this thing stuck
like a whinbush in the gap of his throat.

STONE

A good drystone wall knows where it stands
and, what's more, it knows what it is: it belongs.
It has character and strength and it wears
its years well: like a castle or a cathedral.
A well-built drystone wall fits itself
as snugly to the landscape as good homespun

does to a man; it rides the townlands like
a boat rides the swell; you can follow it
for miles and miles as it takes the rough
and the smooth in its stride. Certain drystone walls
have been there so long they are bone once more
of the landscape's bone rooted as much

in myth and history as a standing stone.
Sometimes they look like the land giving birth.
One drystone wall I know in Friary
is so fleeced with grass and cushioned with plush
tussocks of moss that you'd be hard put
to catch a glint of stone in it at all

and another I know in Greenans is
so threadbare you can see sky showing through.
In Lough Eske Wood there's a tumble-down
straggle of stones masquerading as wall
through which impudent wrens flicker like tongues
of shadow and stoats thread their sinuous way

and, on a day of rainbows and cloud shadows
you can glimpse something more like
spittle than showers fleetingly speckle
the walls of Ardnamona until you think
it's a new grain in the stone you hadn't
noticed before or instant weathering.

I know there are people round here who think
I'm a bit gone in the head the way
I keep going on about drystone walls but
I could go on for as long, or longer,
about old houses, castles, cathedrals.
What I'm gone in the head about is stone.

FERN

is a copycat arching its back
under the half-hoops of the bramble and, later,
a small child's minuscule bunch-of-bananas hand;
is the crozier of a bishop or
a Viking longship dragon,
the isosceles triangle of isosceles triangles,
a measure of the wind's weight in calm weather;
is a fish picked clean to its green bone,
a bonsai Christmas tree pressed paper-thin,
the groundling's answer to the freedom of the feather,
the wing of a malingering plover
or a Gothic window grille of rusted metal;
is osteoporosis of the bracken
whose boneyards I crackle through and
whose ghosts begin to haunt window panes
in the first hard frosts of late autumn.

PICKING MUSHROOMS

Look how they break in your hands like soft chalk or
sacramentally like bread, how sometimes you come
on one the accordion-pleated beams of whose cupola

are enclosed with a thin white membrane and
how if you should happen to put your finger
or your thumb through this gossamer skin

you are suddenly overcome with the sense of
having violated the perfection
of God's handiwork the way it is when

you mar the cloud-crowded radiance
of a beach just glazed by the tide or
a starched sheet of virgin snow

with the print of your feet or
the way it was for a moment once when
the veil of the temple of her body was rent.

FUNERAL

Interminable slaughter and
crippled lives, tribes
and the barbed languages of tribes,
Norseman and Norman,
Planter and Gael,
and the terrible incubus,
history, riding the present,
whispering lies. What more pitiful
than to hear them begging
their God for mercy yet again
under these cold Northern skies?
Look how the closed faces
mirror the closed minds
of the past's masters, setting
hate at the throat
of love even at the edge
of the grave, promising
apotheosis to all in exchange
for the ritual blood sacrifice,
drawing the sting out of death
with moth-eaten battle cries. And this
has gone on for centuries, centuries.

THE MAGIC REALISTS

Tonight, all over this divided city
where people in small terraced houses
are viewing the big gangster movie on BBC,
one family, watching a mobster
riding shot-gun in a stolen car, hears him
come raging through their own front door.

FISHERMEN
for Derek Hill

Who's that dour man with the quarried face and
the gnarled hands lumped in his lap like turnips?
Him? That's Nahor in from the island with
the salmon from last night's big run. Now he's
filling his gut before he goes back out.
Look at the eye of him. Try and plumb it.
Cast your net in him. What'll come up in it?
A decapitated cross, a cursing stone,
the broken images of older gods, shards of
obscure Gaelic. Splash him with God's holy water
and it runs off him like rain off an upturned currach.
The saint was out there once fishing for men?
When he trawled so wide he should've trawled deeper.

THE BLACK SHEEP

Listen. The Angelus bell has begun
to toll faintly in the glen. And look,
over there under a low sky bloated with rain,
a man mending fences who takes off his cap
to no one but God and to eat and sleep,
has suddenly bared his head to pray.
Two dogs lie prostrate like acolytes at his feet.
I know his name and the names of his dogs and
once I broke bread with him in the kitchen
of a womanless house as bare and white
as the limewashed house of his God down the road.
We talked about ewes and wethers and how
he'd been searching for a black sheep he'd lost.
I remember the coil of rusted barbed wire
sitting on the bald skull of a boulder like
a crown of thorns encrusted with dried blood
and the ragged cross on the side of his hill
was the skeleton of a flayed scarecrow marking
the place where a crop had failed and he gave in.
And I remember too how he and his dogs
penned me in a corner of that windswept
kitchen like a sheep that had strayed from
the fold of the crucified Sheepman hanging
like a scarecrow from a nail in the wall.

FIRSTS

for Attracta

I found your mother there and pine martens
in the bens and two basking sharks like cloud
shadows darkening the bay. The busman
arrived at our door one day bristling with
the antennae of a live lobster and
a corncrake clattered away all night long
under our window in the wilderness
of rank grass we called a lawn. They were all

firsts for me and so was the swallow I
saw the following year flashing over
a half door to the nest I knew was cupped
close up against the beam of the roof
like a stoup for the holy water the priest
scooped up into his hand to baptise you.

WORDS AND MUSIC

Even though you're still afraid of horses
and cows I know now, by the way you fill
your jeans and blouse, this doesn't mean you'll take
to your heels and run at the sight of boys. Look
how the sheen of an orange-tip's wing shines
in your hair and, daughter, tall and wind-blown
as that pendulous foxglove by the drystone wall
that needs a bra more urgently than you,
I notice how your eyes change colour
in the light like the distant lake-water
I glimpse through the trees — something surely for
someone, apart from your mother and me,
to dream about now. Who would have thought
to look at you here as we stop by the sign
on the six-foot wall warning trespassers off
that once I watched your mother pat and
powder the small cracked moon of your bare ass
the way she kneads and flours dough to bake
bread or that I know a certain place more
secret and mysterious than even this
clearing in the woods where God when he made you
blew a dimple in your flesh as perfect
as one of those hollows blown here
last winter by the wind in snow? But
it's time to turn back: further than this
fathers, even fathers who are poets,
don't go, and so, my daughter, Orange-tip,
Foxglove, Snow, Lake-water, remember if
you in these woods should one day meet a boy
passionate but, unlike your father, tongue-tied,
tell him you know a poet who has words
for all the tunes that only he can play.

KNOCKNAREA

It was on Knocknarea and there
was no one there but two young
lovers holding hands and this
middle-aged married pair.
A cloud of pollen from some
pines rose into the air like
fine snow and dusted your hair.
We marvelled at a pine cone's
colour and shape, the crusted
lichen on the megalithic stones.
The farms far below us were
toy farms and I wanted to
reach down and move the tiny
lead animals anywhere.
We climbed the cairn and
the lovers got lost somewhere
in the heather. We were
the middle-aged married pair and
the weather was Yeats country weather.

THE LOST FATHERS

To reach the meadow field was just as much
as he could do that day, and there he'd stand
marooned among the archipelagoes
of shadow the copper beech cast on the grass.
I kept my distance — like a dog at heel.
We watched them turning swathes with wooden rakes.
Sometimes he'd wave his stick above his head
at distant figures crinkling in the pools

of rippling heat but no one ever hailed
him now or thought to come and rescue him.
And so, before the women missed him from
his high-backed chair, I'd sidle closer to
this castaway whose hand I wished would reach
for mine the way my father's used to do.

THE DAFFODILS
for Demond MacAvock

You cut them dripping
wet and put them in
a vase

under the Vlaminck print
they breathed life into
the still-life into

the airless room laid out
with the corpses of so
many dead

things I could smell them
in the hall like
birth or

it was like the smell
Lazarus must have smelt
in the tomb

when life took him again
they were breathing
as quietly

as a sleeping child or
someone dying whose breath
will hardly

mist a glass they were
breathing but they were
breathing

their last bleeding
like severed
arteries

aching o aching
for the wholeness
of roots

the daffodils you bled
to death to make
a wound

of colour in this
airless room
their tomb

DIASPORA
for Nik Cohn

Out of a leaden sky at dawn
the falcon falls
all talons on its prey
and under it
everywhere
in death's hushed air
islands
laid out like corpses
in their shrouds of mist.

VULTURE

A sheepman in the Mournes observed it first
gorging on the entrails of a still-born
lamb; next it was disturbed plucking the heart
from an aborted human foetus unborn

for better things elsewhere and on the third
day poachers stoned it from the corpse of an
informer they found gagged with a dragon's turd
and testicles. But it grew weary on

such rich fare, scavenging the abattoirs
of hate until, enormous, gross, and fat
with the viscera of the dove and rat,

sated yet home-sick for the heat and flies,
it bore South again, smelling a sweeter war
where God died long ago of tribal lies.

REFERENDUM

That big drunken man over there
with the twisted mouth starting to sing
Sean South in a tuneless voice,
is that the sheepman whose son was shot?
Aye, that's him. Nahor Devenney of Crieve
a stroke felled on the side of his own hill
and left lying half a December night that took
the last grain of sweetness out of him.
A hard man. In this very pub the day
before the vote he turned his cold eye on me
and said out of the corner of his crooked
mouth that it was a clean thing to kill Brits
with guns but that he'd take a horsewhip
to any son of his he caught with a condom.

CARGOES

Tory of the waves : of warrior and
saint : Balor's island
and Colmcille's,

swathed in seamist, lists under
its weight of myth and
history : Tau

cross and Fomorian fortress, cursing
stone and round tower, shades
of the Norse

marauders forever riding
the fierce white dragons
of the sound.

A rat will not live on Tory island : on
Colmcille's holy ground : but I
look over

at Ireland : insular too, another
ship listing under its own
constantly-shifting

lethal cargo of myth and history, full of
laughing boys, wood kernes, priests, the rats
in the hold

nosing and sniffing at the corpses of all
the grand warriors
and saints.

THE MEASURE
for Nancy McHugh Yates

There's hardly a better way of doing
nothing than sitting on a Lough Eske wall
speckled with green and orange lichens and
overshadowed by foxgloves four feet tall.

Even better is to teach your children
this art of doing nothing at all
by making them sit at the lake beside
you on top of a lichened drystone wall.

And after all that they'll probably leave
you sitting alone on your Lough Eske wall
with nothing except foxgloves to show you
what they were like when they were four feet tall.

THEOREM

for Johnny Boyle

The smallest field in West Donegal,
half-way between Glenties and Dungloe,
has fine drystone walls but no
gate; the biggest field in West
Donegal — not a stone's throw
away — has a splendid wooden gate but no
walls. I'm not sure what conclusion
I should draw from this — I pondered
the problem all the way to Loughanure —
except perhaps it's a theorem in wood
and stone to prove that a field in
Lettermacaward may be geometrically
defined as either a space with walls and
no gate or as a space with a gate and no walls.
One way or the other, I *know* what they think
of Euclid in Lettermacaward in West Donegal.

STORM PETREL

has spent a lifetime trying to perfect
the technique of being able to walk

on water. He scans the surface of the sea
myopically and keeps dipping his feet

in the waves to test them for the exact
temperature at which faith once sustained

the weight of Peter's body on the Sea
of Galilee forgetting that faith is not

an acquired technique in his unremitting
efforts to live up to a famous name.

THE THUNDERSTORM
for Danea

Your small hand, warm and vulnerable and
beautiful as a wild bird, slipped
out of the way of the storm into the sanctuary
of my hand. Into the nest of my flesh and blood.

Now, in your own time and season, out of the way
of the storm, in the sanctuary of your body,
in the nest of your flesh and blood,
you have cradled a child warm and
vulnerable and beautiful as a wild bird.

NEW POEMS

WHALES AT ST. JOHN'S POINT
for Joan

It was all sea and sky out there that day.
It always is. You were with me and we
were in our element rediscovering
the elements of water, light, and air.
The skyline was hung with cobwebs of rain;
filaments of gossamer flashed in your hair.
Just another day looking at mountains,
clouds, flowers, until suddenly, abrim,

tidal with wonder, we saw the whales rise
up out of their element into ours.
Out of the mystery of water and myth
into light and air and into what would now
be a history indissolubly
part of the history of you and me.

THE SONG OF BALOR
for Moya Cannon

All night my fierce eye winks at the eye of the storm.
Give me *one* tree that the wind and sea can deform.

They have stripped me of flesh until I am skin and bone.
My voice is the grinding of seastone on seastone.

On reef after reef I bare my teeth at the clouds.
I spit at the sun trawling in shoals of shadows.

You hear more than the sound of the sea in *my* shells.
I have caves in my soul the saint never entered.

THE NAME
for Helen McHugh

Birra or Durnish: a lake near the beach
always white with tussocks of swans.
And one day last summer coming down
past the wooden sluice-gate with you —
the whirr of incoming wild duck,
a shimmer of waders far out at sea —
I found a white flower masting up through moss.
What's that? you asked. Grass of Parnassus, I said
and as soon as I said it the poem began in my head.
So I said it again. And again. Just the name.

SNOW AGAIN

The insect settled like an asterisk
on what I'd written since I rose at dawn
and then flew out through the open window
towards the small print of a bird. A footnote
to nothing on the white page of the lawn.

PRIMROSES

We thought the whole world was at our feet then,
and most of the time it was I suppose.
We scrabbled in the wet mulch of roots
and were eye-level with ox-eye daisies
and lambs, picked the white pith out of elder
sticks the way we picked marrow out of bones
and ran barefoot across webs of moth-eaten
sand, but what we liked most of all, before

we grew away from that ground of wonder,
was finding windfalls in the long grass
of the orchard and in springtime eating
primroses the taste and texture of whose
petals I would instantly recall
on the lips of the first girl I ever kissed.

MNEMONIC

I'll not easily forget Dunlewey today.
And neither will you. Not because
the sun shone on the mountains and the lake
and the first cuckoo was calling beyond
the hill and the whins were scenting the wind
from the scree; not because it was the first
warm day of spring and the blackthorn was
in blossom and the sycamore in bud
and wheatears were pirouetting on stones
and lambs bleating in the fields and people
sitting outside their houses enjoying
the good weather; not because of any
of these things will I remember Dunlewey
today but because, when we walked down towards
the glen together, we both kept talking
for miles and miles of someone we loved
and wishing she knew her way through the world
as surely as all the burns here know
their way to the lake through the heather.

PUFFIN

In memory of D.J.O'Sullivan

Puffin slipped out of the jungle aeons ago
and headed north to join the circus

when it came to town. That was easy for him
because he'd never forgotten how to paint his face

and he didn't have to act to act the clown.
Once he nearly brought the house down when he mistook

certain guyropes for the fattest sand-eels
he'd ever seen. Now he's a troglodyte

helping to raise his young in a hole in the ground.
When he's not doing that he's sitting sedately

among pin-cushion sea-pinks and shaggy rocks
on the edges of cliffs with thousand-foot drops.

Whatever you do don't put him in a cage
and think if you feed him nuts instead of fish

that he'll begin to scream "Bloody Hell!"
out of a corner of that multicoloured

neolithic axehead he calls a mouth
or rasp out other obscenities he must have picked up

down south from some foul-tongued first mate
of a buccaneer's ship in the Caribbean.

And then there's that walk. Is it a sailor's gait
or is he just camping it up? Puffin's a queer auk.

DEATH'S DOOR
for Cathal Ó Searcaigh

Whatever it is, it's hardly the weather
keeps drawing me back to places like these:
a rock in the sea, a tarn in the sky,
a glen where nobody lives anymore
and where, if you shout there in English, you'll hear
the echo in Irish haunting your ear,
and, today, the side of a hill at the end
of a track — there was never a road —
near a bush and some broken-down walls
under a sky that's sagged so low
it's begun to snag on the cairn of the croagh.
I enter what's left of the roofless house
through the doorless doorway in the first spits of rain.
The jambs and the lintel have rotted away
and it's been open house here for lambs and ewes
since the night years ago the door was unhinged
to help the man of the house down his own
mountainside on the broad of his back.
I stand on the grass of the bedroom floor
waiting for the old whinbush to make
a sound I hear most times I come up here.
Listen. There it is. The creak of a door.

BESTIARY

Nights and he empties himself of himself.
The dregs. All that's left of him now. What used
to wither away and die in the furrows of her flesh
now withers away and dies on the sheet
he didn't wash for weeks after she died.
He tents the bedclothes with his upraised knees,
lifts the edge of the coverlet and sheet,
but all he can smell is the reek of himself: bad seed.
You are different he hears the priest say,
you are not a pig or a cow or a sheep,
but remembers how they found the body
of Owney Ban curled up under a whinbush
like a beast that had crawled away
into a dark place to lie down and die.
He took her for granted. Like God or the rain.
Now all he can do is bury his head
in her clothes like one of his bitches
and sniff at armpits, crotches. Again and again.

INTO THE DEPTHS

Up here on this sunlit headland lambs lie
in the hollows like tiny drifts of late snow.

I am sitting on a rock looking down
into the depths of the sea when I notice

something crossing the dunes with an airborne
float in tow. Something that's coming at speed

up a path on the face of the cliff.
Something I thought at first was a dog

that's stopping dead in its tracks at my feet
and is suddenly eye-to-eye with me

until I can see into the I of an eye
that never looked out of the eye of a dog.

I am sitting on a rock looking down
into the depths in the eyes of a fox.

LOVE AND WAR

Beside this Ulster road flanked
with grass banks and summer flowers
the print of last night's lovers
brings the soldiers running running.

THE RING

It's gold. Engraved with her initials and a date.
She told me who he was and how that dream
of love had come to nothing in the end.
And why she wore it still and always would.
But love, that feeds, renews itself so much
on touch, on kisses and on hands, feeds
on love's memories too, has no beginning
and no end in human hearts, is always there
as it was there that summer day when she
plunged in to save a younger playmate who
was drowning in a pool below the Falls.
They're both long dead but I'm still here and I now wear
her ring. The ring I'd not be here to wear
if love had failed a drowning girl that day.
Love and those hands one of whose fingers wore
the ring my mother's sister used to wear.

THE SCARECROW

In memory of Simone Weil

Sun, rain, snow, storm; the derision of crows;
God letting the world be what the world is;
the children of the children we fed
on a diet of stones with nothing
to throw at me now but the stones of their hearts.
Such weathers have reduced me to this:
a clown's trousers and a clawhammer coat,
my soul slowly beginning to leak
into the boghole at my feet. God knows when
the bliss of all this affliction will end
and the wind finally strip me of my rags
and lay me out on the ground in my shroud
of mist. Then you will know who I am and why
I wore the clothes of the creature called man.
I was made in the shape of a cross.

THE GHOST IN THE MACHINE: A HAUNTING

ARMS AND THE MAN

I loved the sounds before I knew the sense:
Pax Domini sit semper vobiscum.
Surpliced and soutaned, kneeling at the foot
of the altar beside the sanctus bell
and sing-songing the responses, I thought
of a language of pure love reserved for God.
Then I read Virgil, who sang arms and the man
and who would never have heard tell of Him.

No more than that youth they've just discovered
dead might have heard tell of the poet whose
Aeneas gave his grandfather his name
and who took Dante on a guided tour
of Hell. They found his naked body, marked
with burns from an inferno, dumped on waste ground.

METAMORPHOSES

I helped to vest him in the sacristy
and now, the metamorphosis complete,
a bird of paradise had risen out
of the ashes of a crow. And surely
it was paradise he was catching glimpses of
behind closed eyes as I watched him withdraw
into the mystery of a world you
cannot enter with the world in your heart.

Hoc est enim corpus meum. He held
Christ's body between forefinger and thumb
but I was eye-level with two frayed black
trouser-ends and a pair of lumpish boots
and I could not stop thinking of the way
the world is bread and wine and feet of clay.

GOOD FRIDAY

Love in abeyance. Godforsakenness.
Ships of the soul stricken, foundering fast;
the statues shrouded, the altar stripped,
the doors of the tenantless tabernacle
thrown wide open and the church suddenly
bare and Protestant as an unfurnished
room in an unoccupied house with me
praying for the old tenant to return

and for love too and the lights of candles,
an altar fragrant again with spring flowers,
the mystery of veils, closed golden doors,
and the joy of glimpsing the risen Christ
coming down the aisle to show Simon Peter
the prints of the nails in his hands and feet.

THE DARKNESS

Pride, covetousness, lust, gluttony, envy,
anger and sloth: I knew they were all sins
but when I opened the door into the darkness
of the confessional I was in the dark
about most of them. Except the one
that slept coiled up in the darkness of flesh
and would not let my soul burst into flower
again until he'd absolved me and the world

was suddenly light, wonder, Chagall and Blake,
was towers of ivory, houses of gold,
and I was breaking out of the field
of sin's gravity and, buoyant with joy,
afloat in space like a levitating saint
on the terrible thermal of God's grace.

THE MISSION

They had one-track minds and declamatory hands;
they were superb actors in a dying
histrionic tradition not unaware
of the dramatic impact of a black
biretta flourished above a bowed head.
They strode like soldiers into embattled
pulpits and wore crucifixes like swords
at their waists. Their invocations were

trumpet calls to battle against the world
the flesh and the devil and the candle
in my hands could have been a faggot lit
to burn another heretic. They flushed
sin from the coverts of my soul with fear.
Where was love hiding if it wasn't here?

INCUBUS

I lay sleepless. The room was dark as sin.
Nothing astir outside or in except
the mind of God that never rests and mine
bestraddled by the incubus of thought
that some nights rides from hell. Once, heaven stood
by this bed, invincibly it seemed, but now
was only fear of death: the mystery no one
solves or fails to solve without at first being dead.

What could I set against the dark except
that I was still haunted by a ghost
in a machine? The son of God, never
so much himself as on the cross, cried out:
My God, my God, why have you forsaken me?
Who speaks his mind when his heart's in his mouth?

THE BOOK

I turned over my soul. It wasn't there.
I found an angel embattled under the sin
of lust. Its wings were bespattered and it
was gasping for breath in the foetid air.
So I sat outside the walls of the city
and waited for someone to come with bells
ringing and singing to open the narrow gate
and welcome me back in. And no one did.

And so I learned how to live alone
in the desert of matter and dream
of the book that's kept for registering
sparrows, hairs of the head, even the creatures
that crawl out from under atoms and spit: *Where
do you think you'll find your name indexed there?*

HAIL AND FAREWELL

The big bull calf, all sea legs after nine
months afloat, was in his element now,
gorging himself less on milk than on mouthfuls
of fresh air, making a stir in the world
he'd just entered with something still a long way
from a roar, but all I could think of was
my mother's brother setting sail alone
on his voyage earlier that day,

his face a Belsen spectre of skin and bone,
his body invisible in the folds
of the bedclothes, and me listening to him
grinding out the last sound he'd ever make
in this world from the depths of his throat like stones
scraping the keel as Charon launched his boat.

CONSIDER

Consider the unblinking perfection
of this utterly pitiless eye.
An eye being an eye to the heart of a stone.

Consider an eye that has never shed a tear
for being what it is and for what others are.
Consider a piece of matter ground out of a glacier.

Consider the eye of this falcon and the world as it is
and the eye of God flinching at the peephole of a star.

SURRENDER

In the blue distance a wisp of migrant
wild geese; sheep and sheep-droppings; daffodil clumps
in the close-cropped grass above the sea. I am

lying half-asleep on a bed of last year's
crackling bracken with Muckish at my back
and at my feet a rucked and pleated strand.

The sheep scatter: someone behind the hill
is attacking me with volleys of dry sheepdung.
I know it is you come to return me

to the holy ground of childhood, to clay
and roots and walking with God through incense
and flowers. I know you will not leave me

alone as over the hill you come running
towards me, laughing, still firing sporadic volleys.
I surrender to love by returning its fire.

THE BIOGRAPHER: THE LIFE AND THE WORK

His best friend told him that he'd picked his nose,
liked fresh well-buttered bread without a crust,
wore socks in bed when he made love to Mags
and loved to eat the crud between his toes.

A man obsessed with innocence and lust,
romantic passion for a rich old bags,
master of the lyric who thought in prose:
this was someone he knew the way God knows.

Or so he thought until, purely by chance,
the truth emerged: this man made his living
out of telling lies and all he'd learned
from Mags and from his letters and his books,
 and what he'd told his wife and she'd told him,
was art and not the story of his life.

THE SEA WIND

We were the grand-parents doing our best to keep
up with both of you that April-minted day

under a clouded sky tinted faintly blue.
But not as blue as what in the distance we thought

were glimpses of the sea until we discovered they were
pools of bluebells awash among the trees.

You ran, we followed and kept calling you back
as you set the forest cloisters echoing with your shouts.

And then a sea wind suddenly carried the sound
of your voices away among the flowers with us still

trying hard to keep up before it carried away ours.

THE SEA
for Frank Galligan

I know him. And I know his fields
and the way his stony acres are always
the last to turn green in the spring:
he lives on the wrong side of the hill.
I know that shape in the furrows at twilight too:
once tall and straight as his own scarecrow
but bent now under the weight
of a wind that will never relent.
And he knows me and my strange ways:
watching out for birds, stooping
down to look at a wild flower,
sitting under a tree with a welter
of words swirling round in my head.
So there. We know each other. For years.
And always we stop to talk about crops
and weather across stone walls
or ditches or across the burn
that's wider and deeper than the sea
separating the man I know
from the man that knows me.

A PLACE
for Jocelyn Braddell

Not the sort of place where you'll find daffodils
being harried by the winds of March or tides
of bluebells swelling coppices in May,
not that sort of picturesque place at all,
but one of those places where you can be yourself,
can simply be at ease with what you are
by just being there and opening your eyes and breathing air;
a flat anonymous commonplace space
where nothing dramatic ever happens
except that the sunshine so often keeps
losing out to showers and there's not a beach
or a scenic mountain anywhere in sight;
a place to which the tourists never come
even in good weather because it's not
the sort of place tourists are ever
expected to go and where a bleached skull
is all that's left of a blackface ewe
that died there last summer beside the cracked rock
in the heather that's always wedged with shadow;
one of those places beyond all knowing and telling
with as much of a claim to being places
as Errigal, Glenveagh or Slieve League,
an empty desolate nameless space dense
with ordinariness and deity.

THE SHEETS

He did it in the dark: that handsome face,
a gargoyle to her now, grimacing above her.
Some nights it was hands: his paws on her;
hers suddenly paralysed; some nights teeth:
his on the nape of her neck; hers gnashing.
Daddy, she'd try, *Daddy, stop, stop, it's your Flossie!*
Her arms stretched out under him like a cross.

And morning would come with maybe the birds
singing or the shadows of trees dancing
on the ceiling and the Sacred Heart and sheets
her mother had made with her own hands that she'd
now have to wash and scrub until they were
as clean and white as her soul had once been.

133

MAKING SPACE

They came today and I made space for them
among all these letters, manuscripts and books
the way I used to make space here years ago
for their mothers because making space
is one of the things people who love
one another always do. And now it's
coming near the time for someone
to start thinking of making space somewhere for me.
Wherever that is I'm sure it will be
as private and as resonantly silent
as this place here has turned out to be.
But it's not something anyone here mentions
much to me, nor I to them, not even after
what happened some time ago and the doctor came.
A place I never gave much thought to
when their mothers were young.
Or when their children were here today and sang a song.
Only afterwards when they were gone.

THE SWEENEYIAD

Sweeney was full of it and long before
the Brits came and made Brit-bashing the name
of the game he was getting good mileage
out of Ireland's bloodymindedness:
the cold and wet, the stones and the thorns,
no place to lay his head, an enemy
behind every bush, tears as big as cloudbursts
coursing down his cheeks, fantasising
about women in the fork of a tree, going
on endlessly about his wretchedness
to a growing audience of starving fleas
he had to be careful not to incommode
in case they might decide to move house
and reduce his capacity for suffering more;
his head full of grievances and sodden lice
and romantic clap-trap about heritage sites
he had probably littered with kitchen
refuse and mounds of you-know-what;
yapping about beauty spots he'd seen
only once through poitin-tinted mists
and always the agony wasn't quite
agonising enough to satisfy
his superhuman capacity
for lamentation and pitying himself.

O Sweeney, Sweeney, how you loved the whining note —
Alas the day! Ochon! Woe is me! —
how you'd love to be around here now
doing your best to enrage the Celtic Tiger
by fuelling fires and boiling pots and trying
to ensure each of us should know who
he is against and what he is not

by wallowing in the wallow-holes
provided by the State to keep us from thinking
of the state we're in and convince Brussels
that a brand-new CAP should immediately begin!

Birdman, treeman, whinger, masochist, nut,
praiser of the past and everything that's not,
come down from your roost, *do* something for a change,
and we'll send you into Europe with a begging bowl
as dirty and capacious as the Irish Sea.
O Sweeney, Sweeney, you true-born Irishman,
give them ochons and the poor mouth as only you can!

NEWS OF THE NEW WORLD

Peace was too easy: how could this long-haired
one ever exchange his gun for a well-sprung
tart, grow fat-assed sitting in a chair,
die in bed; how could he ever close his heart
against their sad closed faces? In a land
impenetrable and dark as their minds,
far beyond the stridulant insects
and the fierce metallic rasping of the birds,
he heard the plotters in the static
of his dreams and when he woke at dawn he
saw a serpent's flickering specious tongue
withdraw behind their suddenly venomous eyes.

NEWS OF THE OLD WORLD

At last peace came: the vultures, gorged, retired
from the feast but deep in the bush children
still died like flies. At once the victor, tired
but jubilant, accused a second foreign
power of infiltrating excess food
and issued orders for a numbered Swiss
bank account and fully automatic brand-
new bullet-proof Rolls Royce in gold for Miss

Eurasia and himself. And all went well
until a bomb exploded in his Hall
of Heavenly Fame. They swept his jackals
from the corridors of power, the children
died once more, and when they led him from his cell
the vultures stirred: they smelt a dying lion.

MOUNTAINS

Ben Bulben's rucks and pleats, my own Slieve League
shimmering in seamist across the bay:
I saw them through a haze of grief that day
as we drove at speed through Sligo into Mayo
but found we were too late when we arrived.
The nuns had laid her out in cottons and linens
that matched the pallor of her hands and face.
I kissed her cheek and burned my lips on ice
and shed my tears and touched the lidded eyes.
Whatever final image of the world was locked
in there was locked in there forever now.
It was not one of me. Through the window
I could see Nephin sailing out of a cloud.
Not an image she'd ever have wanted to see
after listening so often to me going
on about going up mountains when she'd
always hated the bleakness of high ground
yet found herself there alone in the end.
And higher than I'd ever been. And needing
love's oxygen to help her to breathe
in that thin mountain air. And none there.
And mist coming down fast everywhere.

BOGSPEAK

For centuries I have been quaking
under the weight of well-shod feet.
None of them was capable of learning
that whoever walks on me walks on water.
If they put a foot wrong they drowned
in what only the wood-kerne knew was
bottomless solid ground.
In my fluid and devious
conspiracies with land and water
I have swallowed stepping stones
the way I have swallowed dolmens and crosses.
I thrive on the liquid diet
martyrdom has prescribed
for the saint and the hunger striker
and, carnivorous too like my daughter
the sundew, I sometimes regurgitate
the corpse of some informer I reluctantly ate.
Now and then the mist lifts to reveal
the substance of my fantasies dissolving
in sunlight but only for a moment
and soon I am fantasising again.
Enter me gently and never forget
what my loneliness masks: all my dreams are wet
and I keep coming under the pressure
of alien bodies I love to hate.

Sometimes with the sun's help I crack a dry joke.
Mostly I've been going up in puffs of smoke.
Bog-man, bog-bishop, bog-job:
I have a bad name: as many
as there are different kinds of wet weather
in the taxonomy of rain.
I flow slow and run deep: the lie of the land.

In summer you can hear me ticking
over like a clacking hen sitting
on the clutch of bombs
history lays and hatred slowly hatches.

SWANS

come in at the ends of their tethers
lamenting like the Children of Lir
at their fate before they drown

their sorrows in the waters of the lake;
then have the neck to try and show us
that what we thought was a ramrod in flight

a few moments ago is really an s-bend
pipe that unbends and plumbs itself
to the bottom when they alight;

take to the land and shatter all the dreams
we ever had of ballerinas and *Swan Lake*;
watch the off-white waterfall

turn green with envy in the sea
but know it will have its revenge
when their cygnets first see the light of day;

are reputed to find their *real* voices
not long before the end and sing
the songs they're always dying to sing.

ESTRANGEMENT

Grass still bent under the weight
of yesterday's rain;
black turds

of slugs; the white flash of birds
far out at sea
like flurries

of purposeful snow and you,
withdrawn and inviolable
this morning

as the mountain in its habit
of mist, your eyes opaque
with distance,

the sea on my lips salt
as last night's
tide of tears.

VIEWING THE RUINS

Under creased tea-stained tissue-paper skin
the veins on the backs of his hands

surface like the gnarled roots of old trees.
When he rises from a chair or climbs the stairs

he creaks and whistles like the timbers
and rigging of a ship in a storm at sea.

The child that he was is the ghost beginning
to haunt the ruins he thinks is a man.

I watch the old growing old by watching myself.

BIRCHES

Birches in leaf are girls
in their summer dresses.
Even in winter they remain
different: they strip
better and their skin
gleams after rain.
They stand naked
and unashamed, frail
as porcelain, and utterly
feminine.

FOXGLOVES
for Matthew Sweeney

went topless long before it was
fashionable and let all hang

out shamelessly over grass banks
and low stone walls like harlots leaning

over their half-doors. They're plastered
with rouge and weighed down with as many

love-bitten breasts as the statue
of a crumbling eastern goddess —

and look how each one of them's mottled
with beauty spots like a trout!

But it's all up front, there's nothing behind:
when they're past it and poxed

and wasting away you can see
they were mostly vertebrae.

A POEM FOR KIERAN

that he may always find wonder
in a clutch of eggs in a wildbird's nest
or the print the hare left last night in the long grass
and dream of some day finding a mermaid's
love letter in a beached bottle
with kisses like starfish shining on every page.

LOVE AND PEACE

My daughter painted the words
LOVE and PEACE on our crumbless
bird-table. I suspect that birds are
illiterate and in favour

of brash aggression; certainly,
being sometimes near starvation,
they'd hardly relish the irony
in this moral exhortation.

Crumbs, not words, are strictly for the birds.

DRYAD

The sounds and smells of felling. And then we came
on the fellers and on the toppled
trunks and scattered limbs of all these trees
that not long ago had cradled birds
and clutched at the skirts of clouds
but now lay like slaughtered innocents
on a battlefield. It was the fate of one
that moved us most: a birch tall and slender
as our eldest daughter and the only
birch among these groves of conifers.
Its peeling bark was the exact shade
of a horse chestnut before the light
darkens it and yellows the white velvet
mould into which it was poured.
At the merest touch of the saw's teeth it
toppled to the ground and something
that was neither a leaf nor a leaf's shadow nor a bird
fluttered out of its foliage and disappeared.
What was that, you asked, was it a bird?
But I had nothing to say, not a word.

EPISTEMOLOGY

She is singing to herself in the kitchen.
A song about youth and love. Age has not
yet sucked all the sweetness out of a voice

that reaches me faintly as I lie in bed
reading in the room above. I listen.
A new note has crept into her voice

and suddenly a stranger is singing the song
in a way I'd never heard her sing it before.
All those years of sharing, of secrets uncovered,

laughter, tears, all those mysteries love
unlocks from the heart kiss by kiss, I knew *her*
but *who* was this? An ageing woman is

singing to herself in the kitchen below while
an ageing man in bed upstairs is reading
Bertrand Russell on how we know what we know.

A CLASSICIST IN THE BLUE STACKS

The day that I went up to Meenaguise
and helped to draw some water from Bob's well

and Bob began to talk of Plato's Greek
that would have been all Greek to me I knew

I'd come as close as I would ever come
to something like a source because when you

go drawing water from Bob Bernen's well
you're drawing more than water from a well.

DOWSING
for Caitríona McNamara

There is something going on here today
that was not going on here yesterday,

the stir of some subterranean force
as, the pen in my hand poised over the paper

like a hazel rod in the hands of a dowser,
I am suddenly brimming over

with the mystery of words that lie
far deeper underground than water

yet come spurting up until I plug
their flow with this full stop.

ST. COLUMB'S

in memoriam Derek Hill

A house as full of subtle light and shade
as one of the pictures hanging on its walls
smoulders like a Monet poppy among trees
and the shadows of trees. The blue
of the hall is the blue of a god's eye
and the lake borrows and ruffles the blue
of the sky. Two horse-chestnuts gravely
acknowledge the breeze and I acknowledge
the Berensonian eye for beauty
that has been at work here as sedulously
as these bees at work among the peonies.
And suddenly I have a sense of someone
from Parnassus waiting in the wings
to announce a dance of nymphs and fauns
around the slender white columns growing on the lawn.

A POEM FOR GARBHAN

that he may one day find enlightenment
in deciphering the symbols gulls print
on the beach with their feet and love
in the sweet nothings larks make into songs
to storm heaven with all day long.

In Memory of Lawson Burch 1937-1999

Ardara, Glenties, Rosbeg, Narin, Portnoo:
those were your favourite stamping grounds.
You knew where you stood when you stood there.
And whether you were one of the throng in Nancy's,
a glass in your hand, that glint in your eye
maybe hinting at some new story on the way,
or paying your tributes in painterly skill
to the Master himself of your art and mine
by making your own world lit with your own light
on canvases as bare and white as the void could have been,
I knew you were always drawn to the high ground.
And that's what you always found around here
and suddenly walked right through the arch
of a rainbow still wet with a paint
you'd had your eye on for years in the glens
and never wanted to walk back out again.
I can guess what you said to the Master up there.
What sort of a brush do you think I should use on thin air?